# HOW DOES
# YOUR
# GARDEN GROW?
# by MARY

Barrington, Rhode Island
1995

ISBN  0-9649466-0-2

*Edited by:* Alexandra M. Cutler
Office of the publisher:
Mary and Me
5 Mathewson Lane
Barrington, Rhode Island 02806

First Printing May 1973
Fourteenth printing October 1995

Printed in the United States of America
By E. A. Johnson Company, East Providence, Rhode Island

# FORWARD

In a day when plant lovers are increasingly sophisticated, when they flip off polysyllabic names of garden chemicals and use latin names for plants with ease and equanimity, and know the botanical families to which belong many cherished flowers, it is indeed refreshing to take in hand a delightful spoof such as this book provides.

Inspired in childhood by original sketches in her Grandmother's Pittsburgh home, drawn and captioned by that genius of nonsense, Edward Lear, Mary Hilliard Jackson sought to capture the wit and fun she found throughout the fabric of botanical pedantry. From childhood she knew of the nonsense verse and prose of England's Edward Lear: *The Owl and the Pussycat,* his masterful never-naughty limericks, and his four *Nonsense* books for children and second childhoods. Copies of these books are rare indeed–rare because they were so loved by all that they were lost through use and reuse, worn out, gone. His three volumes entitled *Nonsense Songs, Stories, Botany,* and *Alphabets* are also collectors items today. In each volume, the botany section of a dozen or so leaves devoted each page to a simple sketch of a wholly imaginative plant or flower with a two-word all-nonsense descriptive caption, such as "Tigerlillia Terribilis" [a lilyform flower with tiny tigers for petals], or "Polybirida [a parrot] singularis."

These were the sketches that inspired Mary's garden. In a few instances we find that she has aped or paraphrased Lear, as with Nasticreechia Krawluppia from Lear's "Nasticreechia Krorluppia," Ticktockia from his "Tickia," and for the pansy she unabashedly adopted Lear's own Phattfacia but with a delightfully gay descriptive extrapolation for the non-juvenile that Lear would never have penned to paper. Most of her plants, however, are drawn for her own pleasure, and yours. Her style is her own as are the nonsensical family sobriquets to supplement the pseudo-latinity of the binomials. To these she has injected wit and humor through descriptive guides to the reader for better use and appreciation of the subject.

You have in hand a pokeyphun book that the plant and flower lover especially will enjoy–and more so after the second reading.

*George H. M. Lawrence*
*10 April 1973*

In preparing the first edition of this book, I was fortunate to have the enthusiastic encouragement of the late George H. M. Lawrence, founding director of the Hunt Institute for Botanical Documentation at Carnegie-Mellon University in Pittsburgh. An eminent botanist and plantsman, he was inspiration not only to his scientific colleagues but to all of us who simply love plants and gardens. He unfailingly respected the layman's interest and was delighted by good natured fun at the expense of pedantry.

Eighteen years have passed since Dr. Lawrence wrote this Foreword, and thirteen since he left us, but its grace still reflects the empathy and humor, as well as the erudition, that I remember with unabated joy.

*M.H.J.*

TICTOKIA                                         (Thyme family)

Does well under glass. Usually spheroid in form, but newer
varieties appear in uncommon shapes. Occasionally found
in pendulous form.

POTOTEA          (Pitcher Plant family)

An old-fashioned garden favorite. Comes to full perfection in late afternoon. Growth is short and stout.

HOTLIAQUATLIA BOTTLIA                    (Sacciforma family)

This plant is used to greatest advantage for cold frames and hot beds.

CONIA MULTIFLAVORA                    (Freezia family)

Offers wide range of color and form to suit every taste. Available year round but outstanding in summer. A truly delectable plant.

BURDIBUSH                                    (Egginestia family)

Feathery florets form lively clusters of golden trillers which should be epiphytic. Cheap.

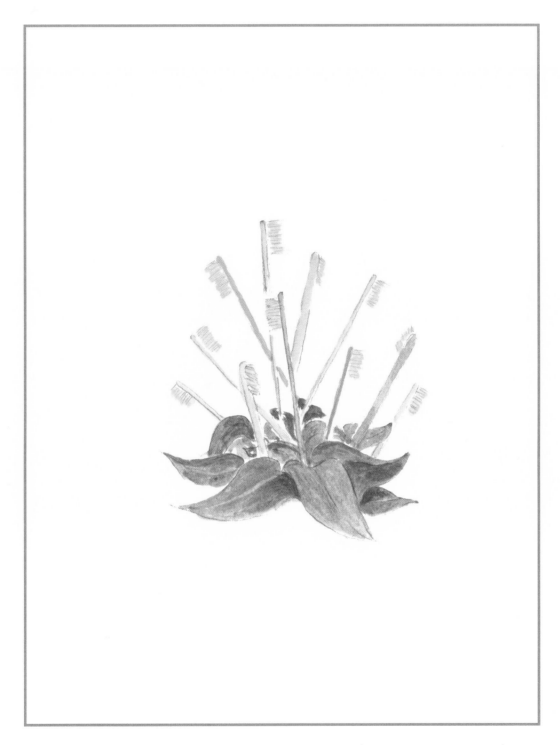

MULTIDENTLIA FAMILIA                    (Cuspidorum family)

Should be plucked daily and watered liberally. Does not take
kindly to transplanting.

POLISITTA CIRCULATA                                 POLISITTA ALLALONA

The polisittas are exotic, showy members of the notorious Wanacraka family. Both species make a vivid display. Prefer sunny location.

PACIFIRE PENDULATA                    (Cowbane family)

A familiar and important nursery plant. Bulbous stamen
protrudes conspicuously from rubbery corolla. Plant near
Dwarf Humani.

NASTICREECHIA KRAWLUPIA (Calamutus family)

Sometimes jocularly referred to as "the moveable feast." This plant does indeed convey the feeling of motion as the furry little tendrils undulate on the peduncle.

PISCI ODOROSA                    (Physh family)

Usually found in wet situations. Blossom has slightly scaly texture. Not suitable for long-lasting arrangements.

HIPPIOSIS VULGARIS                    (Squalidum family)

Both male and female of species exceedingly piliferous.
Indifferent to soil conditions and exceptionally well adapted
to pot culture.

MENIMUTTSIUM                                    (Phox family)

Domesticated form of Phox. Unique bark. Frequently
requires staking and must be fed and watered daily. Very
fertile. Tends to be prolific. Innumerable hybrid species.

VERIDIS CRISPIS                    (Splurge family)

Among the more difficult annuals. Judicious pinching may encourage growth, but considerable loss may be expected each year. Classed as tender.

Femina erecta                    (Ladywort family)

Somewhat lacking in grace and beauty, but a strong bloomer
of robust habit. Seldom prostrate.

OPEN BUKIA                                    (Reed family)

Among the most intriguing of plants. Demands good light and
concentrated attention. Leaves turn with maturity.

PHATTFACIA                                    (Pansy family)

A colorful addition to the gay garden. Prefers bedding among
own kind. Usually found in pairs.

BALLONTEA                                    (Mulligan family)

May be planted only under rigidly restricted conditions.
Illegal in wild places. Addictive.

EGOPUSS REX

A rare and imposing specimen for the wild garden. Must be handled with extreme care. A voracious feeder. Dig only when dormant!

SPULATRED                                    (Gusset family)

Modest and unassuming, this plant belongs in every lady's garden. Sow at any season. Makes a fine border.

HORSIASTER                    (Rhode-apple family)

A well-rounded performer. Caudate. Enjoys a generous
shovelfull of manure at regular intervals.

CHERUBI SUBLIMUS                    (Bluyonda family)

Clusters of winsome little fruits. Period of bloom is fleeting, at
peak around Christmas. Alien and heavenly.

GAMMIA VARICOSA

Considerable diversity of form. Should be covered after early
bloom has passed. Successful propagation requires division of
old clumps. Occasionally produces runners.

KUKENTULES                                    ETONTULES

Importance of clean, disease-free plants can hardly be over-
stressed. Both varieties of tule are in widespread use.

FRIDEGGIA                              (Spatulate family)

A sunny little plant which responds with satisfying vigor when
exposed to heat. Transplant carefully when aged.

PLUNGERIA

A somewhat unprepossessing plant but extremely useful in moist situations.

SUMMA KAMPAS                              (Foetidus family)

Vigorous developing scions. A robust annual. Forms large clumps.

Christy I have such happy
memories of Your Sunday School day

Helene Johnson

ISBN  0-9649466-0-2     $1